Durham

in old picture postcards

by
June H. Crosby

European Library - Zaltbommel/Netherlands MCMLXXXV

GB   ISBN 90 288 3274 2 / CIP

© 1985 European Library - Zaltbommel/Netherlands

European Library in Zaltbommel/Netherlands publishes among other things the following series:

IN OLD PICTURE POSTCARDS *is a series of books which sets out to show what a particular place looked like and what life was like in Victorian and Edwardian times. A book about virtually every town in the United Kingdom is to be published in this series. By the end of this year about 175 different volumes will have appeared. 1,250 books have already been published devoted to the Netherlands with the title* **In oude ansichten.** *In Germany, Austria and Switzerland 500, 60 and 15 books have been published as* **In alten Ansichten;** *in France by the name* **En cartes postales anciennes** *and in Belgium as* **En cartes postales anciennes** *and/or* **In oude prentkaarten** *150 respectively 400 volumes have been published.*

For further particulars about published or forthcoming books, apply to your bookseller or direct to the publisher.

This edition has been printed and bound by Grafisch Bedrijf De Steigerpoort in Zaltbommel/Netherlands.

PREFACE

The City of Durham is unique in several ways. It is not simply that Durham has the finest Romanesque cathedral in Europe situated on a spectacular peninsular site from which, together with the Norman castle, it visually dominates the city, as it has done since mediaeval times. On a lower level, the river in its own way, because of the remarkable course it takes, has virtually dictated the geography of the town and the pattern and nature of the steep streets.

The relative tranquility of the views of the Market Place presented here disguises the fact that at that time all traffic moving from one side of Durham to the other had to pass through the Market Place. Two of the three roads leaving the Market Place were (and still are) so narrow as for it to be virtually impossible for two vehicles to pass each other. The Market Place could not be avoided by using back streets — there weren't any. This remained true until the new inner through road was completed in the early 1970s.

Durham has a remarkable variety of streets and buildings of all ages. A few of the oldest buildings still have much of their original basic structure little changed, though there may have been later additions. A 14th century monk would have no difficulty in recognising the subjects of a few of these postcards.

But of course Durham has much changed through the centuries, with the development of trades and industries and the accompanying increase in population. There were new buildings and streets as the city grew outwards, with demolition and major alterations as well. In this century slum clearances, or simply demolition of outworn buildings, have obliterated a great deal, sometimes without trace. A striking example is New Elvet, where few buildings more than sixty years old remain.

Perhaps the greatest changes over a short time were those occurring after the Second World War; the University expanded on to land south of the Peninsula, and a new inner road was driven through the city with much demolition which, although it opened up fine views of the city, also destroyed many interesting buildings and streets (fortunately, none on the Peninsula).

Not all of these buildings and streets found themselves on postcards, unfortunately. It has not for example been possible to find a card showing the old Palace Theatre at the bottom of Watergate, where Charles Chaplin once performed as the 'Lancashire Laddie'.

It is surprising how quickly scenes can fade from

one's memory. A few years ago, my husband failed to identify an old street scene until he noticed our house some 200 yards away, on the edge of the picture; we had lived there for some years before the buildings in question had been demolished.

Naturally, in a small historic and visually exciting city like Durham, postcards primarily produced for visitors tended to concentrate on the historic buildings and the splendid views, many of which superficially at any rate have altered little since the date of the cards. A few such have been included here, as they help to set a historical and visual background. But many scenes *have* changed. The Market Place in particular has altered with the replacement of old buildings by large stores such as Woolworths, and the various modifications of the Pant. In other places, views taken now from some of the same points as our cards would show the new through road, the new bridges, the related gaps and areas of demolition, or the new block of the National Savings building challenging the Cathedral in its puny and unpleasant way.

It has not always been possible to give firm dates to the postcards. Where the card has been used, the postmark is obviously a help, but often it has only been possible to give an approximate date from evidence within the picture. A few cards, though clearly within our period, cannot be confidently dated at all.

When I first came to Durham in 1947 the City, as a local government unit, was small, though there was much building (later substantially increased) close outside its boundaries. But with local government reorganisation in 1974 its boundaries were widely extended, and Durham City now includes some nearby villages. Some of these are of considerable interest and I have thought it worth while to include a few cards illustrating them.

Acknowledgements:
My sincere thanks are due to Dr. J.L. Crosby for typing and to Mr. D. Kelly for photographic help. I am also much indebted for the loan of postcards to Dr. C.W. Gibby, to the Dean and Chapter Library, Durham (and especially Mr. R. Norris), to County Durham Library Service (and especially to Mr. S. Dean and Mr. I. Nelson), to Mr. Peter Tindale and to Mrs. D. Ferguson.

Durham from an Aeroplane
(showing Great Loop made by River Wear)

1. This may be the earliest aerial photograph of Durham (1928?). It shows how the Cathedral rock is made almost an island (a peninsula) by the loop of the River Wear. A 17th century writer likened Durham to a crab with the Peninsula as its body. The crab's 'claws' are the roads curving away from the City. The two Elvets (70, 77) divide once Elvet Bridge (just above centre) is crossed. At the top, South Street (69) and Crossgate (63) stretch out from beyond Framwellgate Bridge (7) which is not very clear. Prominent in the foreground Claypath and Gilesgate run roughly parallel to the river. Gilesgate Station, just above the word 'from', was Durham's first railway station in 1844. It has long been closed.

DURHAM, FROM PELAW WOOD.

2. Pelaw Wood was given to the City of Durham by Lord Londonderry earlier this century. From its lovely wooded slopes there is a magnificent view across the river with Cathedral and Castle towering above the roof-tops. The old name for the flat land across the river was 'Smiddyhaughs' (i.e. the riverside fields belonging to the smith). From 1773 to 1887 Smiddyhaughs was the city's horse-racing track. Now it is the University playing fields. Surely there can be no cricket ground in a finer setting anywhere else in the country. Frank Tyson, of England cricketing fame, played here for college and university before he earned the nickname 'Typhoon' by bowling Australia out in 1954/5. Each July the magnificent skyline is the backcloth for the miners' 'Big Meeting' and fair held on these fields. (Photo 1930.)

Durham, The Race Course

3. About 1928. It is one of the delights of Durham that within minutes one can be out of crowded streets and enjoying the wooded banks of the River Wear. This stretch of the river lies below St. Hild's College (42) and Pelaw Wood on the left. On the right is the Race Course, so-called because of the horse-races held for many years on the low-lying land (2). Just off the right of the picture a path turns off sharply and curves round behind the houses at the head of Old Elvet. This turn was known as Tattenham Corner in racing days and was 'the downfall of many a good horse and man and has lost many a race'. The horse-racing finished in 1887, and the stone from the grandstand was used to front a row of small houses at the top of Hallgarth Street.

4. This view also shows Pelaw Wood, but much more distantly than the previous card. The foreground and middle distance have changed greatly since this picture was taken. The roof tops in the right-hand corner, once part of several buildings lining little Paradise Lane which led to the river, have all disappeared. A coach park is there now. The new Leazes Road has carved through the leafy slopes of the former 'Paradise Gardens' below, and destroyed the gardener's cottage by the river. Gone too is the old Baths Bridge seen in the distance; it was replaced by the present concrete one about twenty years ago. Vanished also are many of the buildings on the far side of the river.

5. This partly Regency house (Woodbine Cottage) was a familiar landmark on the river banks near to Baths Bridge until about fifteen years ago when a landslip from beneath the new Leazes Road (built just beyond where the rear fence is shown) rendered it totally unsafe and it had to be demolished. Many Durham children must have missed its going, for the 'sweetie shop' at its far end was a popular port of call on the way to or from the nearby swimming baths. The group of buildings in the trees above include the former St. Nicholas Vicarage and Leazes House which was originally the home of the Henderson carpet manufacturing family and later used by Durham Church of England High School, and Bede College.

6. Elvet Bridge was first built during the episcopacy of Hugh du Puiset, 1153-1195. It stimulated settlement in lower Elvet and, until the 'New Way' below Maiden Castle was destroyed by the river in 1559, was part of a major route south. The bridge was cleared of houses on its north side in 1790 and was widened in 1805 by county bridge surveyor Ignatius Bonomi. Until quite recently Elvet residents spoke of 'going over the water' when going to the city centre. The numbers on the bridge piers are for competitors in England's oldest Regatta, held each June since 1836. (Photo 1927.)

7. Framwellgate Bridge (seen here in 1904) was built around 1128 as part of the relocation of townsfolk to Crossgate after the clearance of dwellings from what is now Palace Green. Only a small part of the first bridge remains, partly hidden, under the left arch; the rest was rebuilt in 1401 after flood damage. The city gateway on the bridge was pulled down in 1760 'for the convenience of carriages'. The many planes of the Castle towering above are echoed here by the old buildings clustered at the foot of Silver Street. The deserted appearance of the bridge is deceptive. For over 800 years, until the new through road was built, this bridge and narrow Silver Street had to carry all traffic coming into Durham from the north.

8. In 1895 severe winter weather meant that the River Wear was covered with deep ice for several weeks. Such weather was sufficiently unusual for a local photographer to record it. The result was this charming 'period' postcard of children, choristers and adults skating below the bare wintry trees near Prebends Bridge.

9. The great north door of the Cathedral was made in the episcopacy of Geoffrey Rufus (1130-1140). It was and still is the main secular door to the monastery church and is famous for its sanctuary knocker. Until the Reformation two monks were on duty day and night in a small room above the door ready to admit any fugitives. In 1915 the northern suffragettes discussed a plan to damage one of the pillars in the nave to gain publicity for their cause. However, a local suffragette, Connie Jackson, could not support this idea and so dropped a quiet word of warning. An iron outer grille was installed at the north door as a precaution and is still there and locked at night; this postcard pre-dates the incident.

10. The staring image and curling mane of the Sanctuary Knocker seems forbidding rather than welcoming, pagan rather than Christian. It represents the right of sanctuary for the fugitive, a privilege gained by St. Cuthbert's community as early as about 900. The bronze original is now in the Cathedral Treasury while a realistic facsimile grimaces at approaching visitors. To grasp the knocker has long been popular amongst visitors to our city. Even a leading Soviet official posed thus a few years ago; the caption given to his photograph in the Durham County Advertiser is easily imagined. This card was sent to a Fellow of the Society of Antiquaries in 1910 with the message 'De B. has been banging at this knocker all afternoon ordering gins and bitters'.

11. The Cathedral nave dominates a visitor with its sheer size and strength. Happily little altered in character it still gives a vivid impression of the massive Romanesque design completed in 1133. Sunday School teachers of Victorian Durham, so it is said, would take their charges into the Cathedral and, after letting them wonder at the sheer size of it, would then tell them that Noah's Ark was even longer than the total length of this great Cathedral. The Ark was 300 scriptural cubits long, the Cathedral only 256 (469 feet 6 inches). This probably did little to enhance the children's appreciation of the Cathedral, but it must surely have affected most powerfully their mental image of Noah's Ark. (Photo 1928.)

Durham Cathedral.
Interior.

12. 'A font not to be parallel'd in our land ... carved with such joyners worke as makes all beholders thereof to admire.' So a soldier described the Cathedral's ancient font in 1634. Alas, the font was destroyed by the Scots in their occupation of the city during the Anglo-Scottish war of 1640-1647. A new font was installed in 1663 in the time of Bishop Cosin and Dean Sudbury. Its magnificent canopy, seen here in 1904, is in the part gothic, part baroque style so favoured by Cosin. The simple but elegant white marble font designed to stand beneath is missing, however; in 1846 it was given away as 'unsuitable' and replaced by the clumsy mock Norman font shown here. In 1935 the Cosin font was returned to its rightful place (see 91).

13. This card from 1920 illustrates the Priory gatehouse built by Prior Castell in about 1500 with St. Helen's Chantry Chapel above it. It leads from the Bailey to the green now surrounded by houses of the Cathedral Prebends, but once by the storehouses and offices of the monks. Before the Monastery was closed in the 16th century there was a school for poor children maintained by the Priory. Every day the novices 'left and reserved' part of their food for these 'children of the almery' who were fed in a loft on the north side of this gateway. With the Castle guarding the approach to the Peninsula and this great gateway locked, the mediaeval monastery was highly secure. The tradition of locking it is still continued today.

COLLEGE ARCH,
DURHAM.

PARSONS-NORMAN

14. The central tower of the Cathedral looms above the Prior's Kitchen on the left, the windows of the Monks' Dormitory, and the Deanery whose doorway is discernible on the extreme right. At first sight, this scene of the Cathedral complex from the College seems unchanged. However, the ivy-covered passageway from the Kitchen to the Deanery has gone. The reputation for hospitality and good cooking of the 18th century Dean and Chapter was considerable; how food was kept hot when being conveyed from Kitchen to Deanery is, however, difficult to imagine. The D.L.I. Memorial Garden now shelters between the Deanery and the Kitchen which serves as a repository for archives.

DURHAM CATHEDRAL FROM THE CLOSE

82

15. Bishop Flambard's decision to clear the area between Castle and Cathedral (16) was probably the most significant 'planning decision' in the city's history. For after climbing up the narrow curving hill of Owengate, suddenly there is the dramatic opening out into the light and space of Palace Green and the whole length of the Cathedral is displayed. Although Durham possesses two of these lovely greens (14) neither is called a close as in many Cathedral cities. 'Palace' in 'Palace Green' refers to the Bishop's Palace, the Castle. The people removed from Palace Green were settled in Crossgate and Flambard 'linked the parted banks of the River Wear by building an arched bridge of massive stonework' (7).

The Keep, Durham Castle.

2828. 15.

16. About 1910. A 12th century chronicler wrote: 'The space between the church and the castle which had been occupied with a number of hovels, [Flambard] reduced to a bare and open field, so that the church should be untouched by the contamination of filth or dangers of fire.' The cleared area is Palace Green, seen here looking towards the Castle. While so dominating from the town side, the Castle from Palace Green is less conspicuous. Only the 14th century Keep standing on the Norman motte tries to assert itself. After the troubles of the Civil War the Keep remained in a ruinous state until 1839, when it was restored and adapted to student use by the recently founded University. Debris from the ruinous Keep formed the basis of this raised lawn.

17. This postcard of the procession to the Cathedral to celebrate the coronation of King George V and Queen Mary in 1911 shows a few pieces of vanished Durham. Abbey House, the large building festooned with a swag, remains but has an improved front. To the right beyond the eastern end of the Cathedral is a glimpse of the buildings on the corner of Bow Lane and the Bailey which were demolished to make way for new buildings for St. Chad's College in 1961. The coach house and tiny cottage to the left of Abbey House were demolished when the Pemberton Building was erected in 1931 to provide extra lecture rooms for the University.

Durham Castle   Valentines Series

18. About 1929. The Cathedral's great central tower, 218 feet high, offers splendid views across the city and beyond. This card shows the view northwards across the river where the green fields of Sidegate and Framwelgate stretch up towards the Aykley Heads ridge. The gasometers at their foot belonged to Durham Gas Company, founded in 1824; they were demolished after the Second World War. The skyline is now dominated by the prestigious buildings of County Hall, the Durham Light Infantry Museum, and the County Police Headquarters. Lower down a green belt still survives, stretching towards the National Savings Centre and the busy Milburngate shopping precinct. Crook Hall (just left of St. Nicholas' spire) has a history of nearly 800 years and still survives.

19. 'Gaze on your worthy friend at the Horse's head, and the pretty next [to] him is one of E's cast offs,' wrote the sender of this card of the 1905 Assizes about to set off from the Castle courtyard. H.M. Judges were housed in Durham Castle during the Assizes for 800 years. Their stay has always been the occasion for pomp and ceremony — Assize dinners, a service in the Cathedral and a solemn procession from Castle to Court. Local officers and police still escort the judges but sleek limousines have replaced horse and carriage. During the 1950s complaints from Their Honours about cold quarters and uncomfortable beds produced the idea — quickly quashed — that the Assizes should be held elsewhere. [E. was probably the writer's wife.]

Norman Gallery, Durham Castle

Auty Series. G.H. N/C

20. About 1900. The Norman Gallery was du Puiset's Constable's Hall. The row of graceful columns, zig-zagged arches and window seats together with its feeling of light make it the loveliest room in the Castle. Unfortunately, it was divided into two in the last century – one half left as this wide corridor, the other becoming students' rooms. There is a story of students playing cricket up here one evening in the summer of 1949. A porter came up to complain – the Assize judges were in residence, and might be disturbed. The game resumed. The porter returned, but only to find that a newcomer had joined in the fun – one of H.M. Judges of Assize. The porter quietly went away.

21. Saddler Street still follows its mediaeval route from Market Place to Cathedral and Castle. The Shakespeare Tavern commemorates the fact that this was Durham's 'theatreland'. The first theatre stood by the river facing New Elvet and was reached by the steep steps of aptly named 'Drury Lane' (on the extreme right). Difficulty of access led to a new theatre at street level near Drury Lane in 1791. Then a third, the Theatre Royal, opened behind buildings alongside the inn which became the Shakespeare Tavern. In 1889 this theatre was badly damaged by fire; the gable fell on the tavern, causing much damage. The theatre was partly rebuilt but became a music hall and, later, a saleroom. It was demolished to make way for student accommodation in the 1970s.

Market Square, Durham.

22. About 1913. St. Nicholas' Church was founded in 1133. In pre-Reformation times the Corpus Christi procession started there, as did the weavers' celebration of their patron saint, St. Blaize; civic leaders held their special services there. Patched and altered, the old church survived until it was demolished in 1857 after being weakened beyond repair by demolition of the chancel to widen the road. Monuments and furnishings of over 700 years were destroyed and its graveyard made part of the Market Place. A new church was built and, like the old one, has its tower in the same unusual position on the south wall where it serves as the main entrance. The elegant spire was a happy afterthought of the then vicar.

Market Place, Durham

23. Before 1923. A view looking south from near St. Nicholas Church gives the impression of a late Victorian/Edwardian market square. However, the fronts are misleading, as they mask much earlier building. On the right where the Market Place narrows into Silver Street is Lloyds Bank and next to it the in-fill building on the empty site of 1921 (26). On the right of the card is the Guildhall (25), and beyond it the Market Tavern where the Miners Union was formed in 1871. On the left of the card can be seen part of the dignified and much admired façade of the National Provincial Bank. The Rose and Crown, a hotel which was demolished to make way for Woolworths, is to the right of the Pant, which partly obscures it.

24. About 1895. Shops of today may be functional and hygienic but they often lack the charm of old-fashioned shops such as this one with its handsome and ornate front and packed window display. The Mr. Chapman who is pictured standing in the entrance to 16 Market Place is probably the son or even the grandson of the 'Chapman' above the window, for the shop was established by J.B. Chapman, grocer and seedsman, before 1854, and the shop was still flourishing at the turn of the century. To the right may be seen part of an elegant doorway to William MacFarlane's Rose and Crown Commercial Inn. On the left is part of the entrance to Hutchinson and Greenwell's, wine and spirit merchants.

25. The inside of the Guildhall is very much as it was when rebuilt in 1665 by Bishop Cosin. The original façade was replaced in 1752-1754 by this gothic one donated by George Bowes M.P. Bowes also refurbished the Mayor's Parlour where the panelling still carries the Bowes coat of arms. The Jacobean overmantel in the same parlour was acquired in 1853 from the Red Lion Inn when it became Hatfield Hall. The Guildhall is so much decorated in this card for the coronation of George V and Queen Mary that one can hardly see the balcony from which newly-elected M.P.s still greet their supporters.

Lloyds Bank - June, 1914.

26. Tall narrow buildings are typical of Market Place property where frontage is at a premium. In 1914 this property was given a dignified façade suitable for a bank. Difficulties soon arose. Twice, work had to be pulled down and rebuilt. The side wall was in danger of collapse as the iron supports indicate. In the end all was well and Lloyds Bank and its First World War façade still stands at the head of Silver Street. The mediocre front of the building below the bank masks John Duck's 17th century mansion (65) which had its own water supply piped from the Pant. The heavy timber framing remaining from a building already demolished on the other side of the bank suggests that here too had been a very old building.

27. As the old Pant was demolished in 1863, this photograph must be no later than that year. The Pant had been in a bad state for many years. Around 1815 the pant-masters had replaced rotten pipes with ones which worked even less efficiently. The statue of Neptune, a gift to the City in 1729 from George Bowes M.P., an ancestor of Queen Elizabeth the Queen Mother, was bent nearly double by 1818. A local wit observed that 'Neppy' was trying to dive into the Bowes Arms for a quick drink; so the anchor was installed to prop him upright. 'Honestus' wrote to the local paper complaining about the poor state of the Pant, 'which occasions great delay to servants and tends to debase their morals'. A new Pant was much overdue!

28. It was unthinkable to have no fountain in the Market Place; it was still the only water supply for many people 400 years after its original installation. The decision to have a new Pant was easily made, but nearly three years of quibbling indecision followed before the design of a local architect, E.R. Robson, was accepted. Further discussion followed: should Neptune be added to Robson's design? Some said 't'owd barbarian' should go; others that 't'owd chap' should stay. He stayed and the fountain was installed, but its lighting met public disapproval; Robson had to alter his design again. This card shows the end product. After the 1870 Education Act Robson became a prominent architect of Board Schools. (Photo 1864.)

29. About 1922. A new Pant was erected in the Market Place in 1902; it was paid for with a bequest by a Miss Gibson who lived in the Bailey. Neptune (27) had survived the change once again although his position has been slightly changed. The city was very proud: 'He is truly a dazzling object ... we hope his gay new suit of gilt and bronze is warranted to outlast the winter.' The lovely new Pant and re-furbished Neptune were doomed however, and the reason was traffic pressure which grew very bad in Durham as cars increased, and in 1923 the Pant was demolished and Neptune placed in Wharton Park so that a traffic box could be placed in the Market Place.

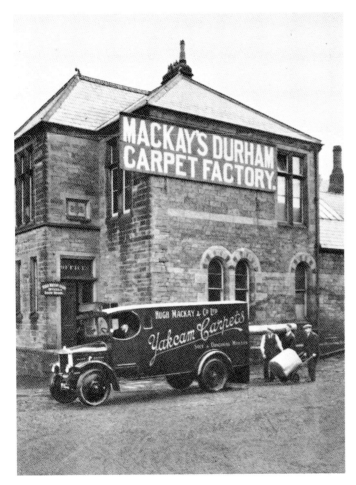

30. Hugh Mackay began his carpet factory in rented accommodation and with hired looms in 1903. The tiny firm prospered. By 1929, when this photograph was taken, it was a sound business concern, exhibiting at the North East Coastal Exhibition. The exhibit included a loom making a Yakcam (Mackay backwards) carpet. The Prince of Wales (later the Duke of Windsor) worked a little on the carpet which was later sold for Cathedral funds. Today the family firm of Mackay still continue the tradition of carpet making in Durham, begun 170 years ago by Gilbert Henderson. It was the take-over and closure of Henderson's firm by Crossley's which left the first Hugh Mackay unemployed and led him to start his own venture.

Auty Series, G.H., W.B., No. 3529

Claypath,

Durham.

31. This charming street, seen here virtually free of traffic, was in fact the only road from the City to the east until the modern through road was built. It is Claypath, one of Durham's oldest streets. There have been many changes since this card was published. The buildings below the Congregational Church of 1893 made way for a cinema (now a bingo hall) and a garage. On the extreme left is the substantial gothicised front of the Gas Company. On the right is C.J. Butterworth's, pawnbrokers, with its three balls. Beyond it is a large bell on a building; does this indicate a public house? Since the new through road was built, Claypath has become somewhat isolated from the City centre, and today appears rather forlorn.

32. The Durham Equitable and Industrial Co-operative Society's main branch occupied a very prominent site in Claypath near the Market Place. It can be seen at the far end in card no. 33. The 'Store' as it was usually called, touched every part of the lives of its members — food, furnishings, insurance, holidays, weddings, funerals and education. The Co-op offered sound goods at fair prices with the additional inducement of a share in the profits by means of the quarterly 'divi' (dividend) for its members, paid out on all one spent. Not a trace of the Claypath store remains now; it was demolished prior to the building of the Claypath underpass.

33. About 1910. This is a reverse view of no. 31, showing Claypath looking towards the Market Place. It is an unusual view for Durham in that it shows two spires which are not common ecclesiastical features in the city. The tall houses mark earlier buildings; there was much infilling and improvement in Edwardian times. On the left is the Mechanics Institute, opened in 1841 with great ceremony; below it a cottage now much altered was the Institute's reading rooms. On the right, the house below the one with an upstairs bay window was Claypath Farm in the 18th and part of the 19th century. Many of the houses have their own wells in the cellar or garden, now disused.

34. The County Grammar School for Girls was opened in 1913 at the foot of Providence Row which leads off Claypath. It was a proud neo-Georgian building indicating the importance the County Council attached to education. It was extended in 1938/39 and again in 1963, and is now part of Gilesgate Comprehensive School. The ploughed appearance of the grounds in front of the school suggests that this photograph may have been taken very soon after completion.

35. Quaint old homes of this type were commonplace (47) in the city until this century when slum clearances of the 1930s and the post-war commercial and road developments virtually wiped them out. This example, in lower Gilesgate, was in 1909 a general dealers and post office. It still had its wooden shutters; its roof is part pantile, part stone slabs. The teapot still survives; it was moved from here to Fowler's the grocers in Claypath, and on demolition of that shop it was moved to its present site outside Martin's the newsagents in Saddler Street. A fine and now rare shop sign, the teapot is now in the care of the City of Durham Trust, the local conservation society.

GILESGATE   DURHAM.

36. This is a view of Gilesgate at the start of its 'second bank'. The foreground has since been transformed by the demolition of the buildings and the construction of the Gilesgate roundabout as part of the major road development. The large stone by the two men on the right is part of a meteorite; its shiny appearance was said to be the result of the local children sliding across it. Removed for safety to St. Giles churchyard during the 1930s, it has since vanished.

GILESGATE DURHAM

37. Gilesgate, as its name indicates, is one of Durham's ancient streets. 'Gate' is derived from a Danish word, 'gata', meaning a street or way. Giles arises from the nearby church dedicated to St. Giles, the patron saint of cripples, and originally the chapel for a hospital founded in 1112. Older residents call Gilesgate 'Gillygat'. Until replaced by the new roads of 1968-1972, Gilesgate was the main road to Bishop Wearmouth, Sunderland and Hartlepool. Behind the houses on the right was Durham's first railway station built 1844; it is no longer used, but G.T. Andrews' station house survives. (Photo 1910.)

38. The Provincial Laundry remained in Durham until long after these elegant horse-drawn vans were in use, but it has now been closed. In the foreground a young lad proudly holds the head of a sturdy pit pony, with its eyes well blinkered. The building in the background is the Vane Tempest Hall, situated behind the south side of the upper part of Gilesgate; it now houses the Gilesgate Community Centre. Originally, it was the Drill Hall of the Durham Light Infantry.

39. The 14th century gatehouse and storage buildings of the former Kepier Hospital are now an unusual farmhouse close to the City centre. It stands alongside the river. The name 'Kepier' comes from a word meaning a weir with a contrivance for catching fish. Traces of the weir still remain. This view of the gatehouse is taken from within the closed area of the former hospital. The hospital reverted to the Crown in the abolition of religious houses of the mid-16th century, and was occupied by several well-known local families beginning with the Heaths.

40. This is the house built in the late 16th century by the Heath family on the former Kepier Hospital lands. Well before the date of this postcard it had been extended and had become the White Bear Inn. The board on the front here calls it the Kepier Inn, which it was until 1892. For about 35 years it was a private house. The building was then largely demolished; a broad balustred staircase and some of the panelling from the hall were removed to another house. Only the south arcade remains; this had probably been built using stone from the former hospital.

Auty Series, G.H.W.

BEDE COLLEGE, DURHAM.

2061

41. A Diocesan School was opened in Framwellgate in 1841 to train men teachers for church schools. In 1847 the neo-Tudor buildings depicted here were erected on Pelaw Leazes for the school. Dignified by the title of Venerable Bede in 1886, the college was united with its sister college (42) in 1976 as the College of St. Hild & St. Bede. Bede's promotion is a little eccentric, as he is not an Anglican saint. In 1979 the college became a university hall of residence and a proud contribution to teacher-training of nearly 140 years was ended. 'The Cathedral' by Sir Hugh Walpole (1884-1941) drew upon his father's experiences while vice-principal of Bede College.

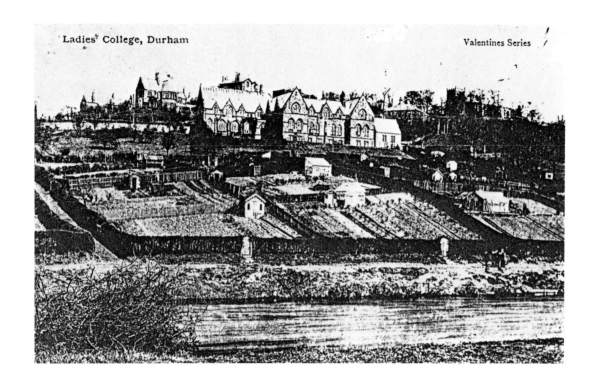

Ladies' College, Durham   Valentines Series

42. Before 1900. A Diocesan Training School for schoolmistresses was founded in 1858 alongside its male counterpart. Built in a commanding position on land once owned by the Cordwainers Guild, it became St. Hild's College in 1896. On the skyline to the left is Manor House and to the right St. Giles Church. Although Victorian, Manor House is rightly named for it was built on land granted to Lord Londonderry as Lord of the Manor when Gilesgate Moor was enclosed. Consecrated in 1112 as the chapel of a hospital founded by Bishop Flambard, St. Giles was once under siege when in 1196 Scottish and English would-be bishops fought for the diocese. It later became the parish church of Gilesgate. The north wall of Flambard's nave still remains.

43. It is very difficult to realise that this mediaeval street was the main street through Durham until about 15 years ago. At its narrowest only 17 feet wide between buildings it had to accommodate both pedestrians and traffic. Although the street line remains the same, as do several of the buildings, there have been many changes. The buildings on the left have been demolished to make way for Marks and Spencer, and the unsympathetic façade of Burtons. The building in the centre of the picture, with its jettied floor, has now been beautifully restored to reveal its timber framing. Buildings in the right foreground have been replaced by new buildings.

44. About 1887. George Greenwell opened his grocery and wine business at no. 2 Silver Street in 1850. A few years later he bought Albert House from its publican, William Marshall. By 1884 the shop had more than doubled in size and the redundant Primitive Methodist Chapel at the back of the premises acquired. A 2-horse-power steam engine had been installed to work three mills for grinding coffee and spices and a sugar breaking machine. Butter was preserved on ice and 50 canisters each holding 100 lbs of tea offered a bewildering variety. Most goods were weighed at the counter. Personal attention was all, and this tradition continued until the firm closed in August 1983. Albert House is now (1985) the city's main post office. This was a publicity postcard.

45. The Castle Hotel in Silver Street stood alongside Moatside Lane (on the extreme left). It was partly demolished as part of the major changes in the city begun twenty years ago. Its fine door head, unfortunately obscured here, was much admired locally and is said to be still in store awaiting re-use. A restaurant and cake shop stand on the site now. The lavish decoration of the hotel was probably occasioned by the North East Cycle Meet of 1909.

46. 'When Coal was King' a Saturday in each July produced a spectacle in the city never to be forgotten by those who saw it. It was 'Big Meeting' day, when the miners' lodges marched into Durham with brass bands and banners, and they and their families took over their County capital. Though there is still a Miners' Day, it is but a pale echo of its great past. On the right of this picture, taken in 1907, beyond Framwellgate Bridge can be seen a terrace of houses which were down by the waterside. This was Lambton Walk, named in honour of Lord Lambton's year as Mayor in 1900. The terrace, with most of the other buildings, was demolished to make way for the new shopping precinct.

47. About 1914. Milburngate was really the lower end of Framwellgate, the ancient road north from the City. When James VI of Scotland made his royal progress south to become James I of England in 1603, he was escorted down Framwellgate and Milburngate and into the City with all pomp and ceremony. Other than the great central tower of the Cathedral crowning the scene, all the buildings depicted have been demolished. The two low cottages in the foreground with pantile roofs have jettied upper stories indicating timber framed buildings of the 16th or 17th century. One is reminded of the comment of Henry VIII's antiquary John Leland who visited Durham about 1535. 'The building of Durham is meetly strong but is neither high or costly work.'

Durham. Milburn Gate.

A backyard; Millburngate.

48. About 1900. Many good spacious buildings of the 18th and early 19th centuries (50) intermingled with lower buildings of earlier periods (51) in Milburngate and Framwellgate. Old photographs of the façades of these buildings may make one wish that they had been retained. Yet a card such as this, with a rare glimpse of the backs of these houses indicates how they had deteriorated into run-down tenements by 1900. Many of the worst houses had vanished by 1939 and had been replaced by neat and hygienic council housing. The remainder, together with that council housing, were demolished in advance of the new road and shopping precinct development.

49. This photograph of Framwellgate, the old coaching road to the north, shows how delapidated and neglected the once good housing had become by the beginning of this century. Framwellgate was replaced as Durham's road north in 1831 by the opening of an improved North Road (52) with a much easier incline. However, the 'new' road north did not prevent, as was hoped, the building of the by-pass from Farewell Hall to Framwellgate Moor. Within the past fifteen years the line of the ancient street of Framwellgate has once more become a major route north from the city, and North Road is largely limited to access traffic and buses. All the buildings seen here no longer exist.

DURHAM CATHEDRAL FROM FRAMWELLGATE

50. Probably before 1914. This distant view of Cathedral and Castle dominating the Durham skyline is still familiar, but all else in the postcard has vanished. Instead, the wide new road to Aykley Heads and thence to Newcastle has taken its place. The gable end facing onto Framwellgate was timber framed. Like other steep Durham streets, Framwellgate was cobbled – a great help to horse and cart in snow or icy weather. For many, the horse age has a romantic flavour, and yet the weary droop of this horse as he eats from his nosebag while resting with his load reminds us of the time when horse power put a tremendous strain on draught animals, not least in hilly Durham.

51. George Blagdon's currier and leather merchant's works was established in 113-115 Framwellgate by 1854. There was still a Blagdon family business there when the buildings vanished in the clearances of the 1960s preparatory to the big changes of the following decade. In front of Blagdon's warehouse are two semi-derelict houses whose jettied upper story and pantile roof suggest an early timber frame building. In the new Milburngate shopping precinct a timber framed building has been retained as a great rarity in the modern development. This postcard and others show that several such buildings survived in the city until relatively recent times.

52. Framwellgate was part of the Great North Road; plans to by-pass the City and avoid using Framwellgate were much opposed locally for fear that trade in the City would suffer. Public protest led to public action. The Mill Burn was diverted into a culvert, land was drained and houses on Framwellgate Bridge demolished to make way for a new improved road north. The upper part of this was called North Road and the lower end (shown here) King Street (both are now known as North Road). The public house on the corner near the 'Five Ways' was called the King William IV, as both it and the road were opened in the year of William's coronation. The public house and adjacent buildings were demolished in the early 1970s prior to extensive redevelopment.

DURHAM. MINERS HALL.

53. This postcard and the next indicate that North Road once had a dignity it now sadly lacks. The old Miners Hall is seen here nearly new with its proud façade still intact and enhanced by iron railings and globular lamps. Next to it are a pleasant pair of stone Georgian style houses; the doorway and window of one have been cut into to allow the insertion of the Miners Hall. In the background is the chimney of Robson's steam corn mill. Since there are only three Sicilian marble statues standing in the niches (those of Alexander MacDonald, William Crawford and W.H. Patterson), this card must pre-date the addition of a fourth, that of John Forman, in about 1906. All four can be seen in card no. 55.

NORTH ROAD. DURHAM.

54. North Road is still dominated by the dome of the former Miners Hall and the distant view of the Cathedral. Much else in the photograph is changed. Robson the millowner's house is now the office of the bus company, and its tall railings and trees have been replaced by mediocre brick buildings, with the bus terminal behind. The Globe Cinema on the other side of the road gave way to a bingo and amusement arcade and then to demolition. This photograph is taken in the opposite direction from that of nos. 52 and 55.

55. This is North Road sometime between 1907 and 1915 looking towards the railway viaduct on which there is a passenger train drawn by a small tank engine, like the one on card no. 61. The old Miners Hall by now has its fourth statue (53). The austere buildings on the right of the card still exist, but the upper windows are somewhat altered and the ground floors have been converted to shops.

56. The 1857 railway viaduct towers over terrace housing below, which the advent of the railway encouraged. The six-horse funeral cortege with the coffin on a gun carrier has a military escort, for it is the funeral of a First World War hero, whose name has not so far been traced. The road is above the floor level of the older building on the right which has a stable type door.

57. The County Hospital looks more like a 17th century Jacobean country house than a Victorian charity hospital. The initiative for building a new hospital to replace the old infirmary built sixty years earlier came from George Waddington, then Dean of Durham; he and other local worthies provided the funds. A London firm, Thompson and Johnson, won the premium offered for the best design and the first patients were admitted in 1853. Admission was gained by obtaining an 'admittance card'; these cards were allocated to subscribers to bestow as they saw fit. The hospital is still there though long part of the National Health Service, but its commanding position at the head of North Road has been obscured by the viaduct of 1857 and by mid-20th century extensions, highly functional but architecturally drab.

58. This is the kind of picture which could puzzle even those who know Durham extremely well. It is an unusual view from Wharton Park looking towards Waddington Street. The lightly gothic Presbyterian Church, erected in 1878, is clearly visible. It backs onto Mowbray Street. But to modern eyes there are gaps. The 'nasty gridiron of mean little houses', as one resident so unkindly described the terrace housing which developed around the railway viaduct before the First World War, was not yet complete. The large open area beyond Waddington Street is the land on which the new Miners Hall was built in 1915, while the ancient Redhills path is clearly visible alongside the poplars. (Photo 1900.)

THE DURHAM MINERS' NEW HALL & AGENTS' HOUSES. OPENED OCT. 23ᴿᴰ 1915.

59. The Durham Miners moved from North Road to their new headquarters in 1915. To the left are the agents' houses. On their right, partly obscured by trees, is the main building designed by a local architect, George Gradon, with a dome echoing that of the earlier Miners Hall (53). The statues from the latter were transferred to the new site; below the trees can be seen the plinths awaiting their arrival. This card was one of a special packet of six sold in 1915 to raise funds for aged miners homes, a project in which the Union was very active.

60. A similar long view is obtainable from just below the railway station today. As always, the Cathedral dominates with the Castle Keep and the spire of St. Nicholas also visible. All the houses in the foreground and the gasometers have gone, as has the tall stack of Blagdon's leather works obscuring part of Framwellgate Bridge. Across the river the old carpet factory no longer dominates the waterfront near the new Milburngate Bridge. After being badly damaged by fire in 1969, the carpet factory (30) moved to new premises and the old factory complex awaits development.

61. Ruskin described this view as one of the seven wonders of the modern world. A superficial glance from the same spot over the roof tops to the ever evident Cathedral and Castle would suggest that little has changed since this photograph of about 1910 was taken. However, much has changed in the buildings nestling below the Cathedral rock. The chimney stacks have gone, and St. Godric's Church (left of centre) acquired a west tower in 1913. Steam trains have been replaced by diesel, and the North Eastern Railway eventually by British Rail. But essentially, in its visual impact, this view is still as Ruskin saw it.

62. About 1900. Apart from its name (derived from the vineyard of the ancient manor of Crossgate), Grape Lane today, with its cheerful homes with 'all mod cons', bears no resemblance to the Grape Lane of nearly ninety years ago. The modern conveniences of this picturesque row were a shared cold-water tap and ash-pit privies. The washerwoman is using the 'washing machine' of her day: a wooden water tub and a 'poss-stick' which was used to pound out dirt from the clothes. Then, the washing would be hung out to dry on a line strung across the narrow cobbled lane. A scene such as this reminds many of us of the quiet washing revolution which has taken place in our lifetime.

63. About 1920. Crossgate affords a magnificent view of the Castle towering above Framwellgate Bridge and the roof-tops of Silver Street. It was the main street of the prior's Manor of Crossgate but, outside the Cathedral archives, hardly a trace remains of the vineyard, orchards, fishponds and tollbooth of the mediaeval manor. St. Margaret's Church (65) among the trees on the right was built as a chapel of ease from St. Oswald's for the manor. It is on higher land alongside an ancient raised pavement reached by steps from the road below. Crossgate kept its semi-rural character until the mid-19th century. Complaints about the nuisance of wandering cattle, pigs and poultry occur in local records from the 16th century until the 1850s.

Durham Castle from Crossgate.

64. This is a reverse view of the preceding card and is a few years later. Most of Crossgate is lined by houses with 18th and 19th century fronts, but behind most of them are traces of much older buildings, one or two timber framed; most have been carefully repaired since the Second World War. This lower end of Crossgate was the 'rough end of the street' in the late 19th century; most of the houses were tenements. The blacksmith was called 'Old Nero, a cognomen more complimentary to him than otherwise'. Behind the smithy was the baker's where 'most had their bread baked and dinners cooked'; it was also 'a place of gossip and frequent shindies'. The barber's shop next door was also a gossip centre — 'a sort of Central News and walking encyclopedia' combined.

65. About 1910. The interior of St. Margaret's retains some of the original features of its 12th century foundation, notably this graceful south arcade of four Norman arches. The further clerestory window is claimed to be the oldest surviving one in the county. In the nave floor there is a memorial to Sir John Duck (died in 1691); he is often called the Dick Whittington of Durham. Despairing of finding fame or fortune in Durham, Duck decided to leave the city. A gold coin dropped by a raven near Framwellgate induced him to 'turn again'. He made a fortune from coal, butchering and other business ventures; he was awarded a baronetcy, became Mayor of Durham and a generous philanthropist whose benefactions included almshouses at Lumley and Duck's Charity in Durham.

ST. MARGARET'S
DURHAM

Old Houses in South Street against the East End of the Church

66. 'The Curtain' is a corner of bygone Durham which has utterly vanished. The half-timbering, jettied floor and pantile roof hint at its great age in this early 20th century postcard. The east window of St. Margaret's Church (65) peeping over the roof indicates an approximate position at the lower end of South Street (69). The Curtain was probably demolished when the area was cleared for the building of the Johnston Technical School (68). The origin of the name Curtain is uncertain. Curtain is sometimes used of a wall connecting two parts of a fortification; this is unlikely here. Curtain may simply mean an encircling wall.

67. About 1901. Apart from the tower of St. Margaret's Church and the steps leading to the river at the west end of Framwellgate Bridge, everything in this card has vanished. The same viewpoint today would show the Coach and Eight in place of the Criterion, and a view of the Public Library and the backs of the housing development at the foot of South Street in place of the huddle of houses. By an odd coincidence, the right-hand side of this card fits almost exactly to the top left-hand side of no. 46.

Saint Margaret's Church, Durham from Framwellgate Bridge.

S 9311   JOHNSTON TECHNICAL SCHOOL, DURHAM.

68. Johnston Technical School at the lower end of South Street (69) was a fine red brick building with Dutch gables erected in 1899. This card shows the original building with children in the playground below, and the large extension of 1906. It was named after James Finlay Weir Johnston whose handsome bequest made its foundation possible. A lecturer at Durham University from 1833 till 1855, he keenly believed in the vital importance of science in education; this was reflected in the school's early curriculum. The school moved to Crossgate Moor in 1952. No trace of the original buildings survives; they were replaced by an expensive housing development which now fronts the lower end of South Street opposite St. Margaret's Church.

69. Today, property in South Street is very 'up market'; a judge, eminent architect and other professional families live there, and the façades are beautifully maintained. But the origins of South Street were much more humble. Street directories of the 19th century reveal a street of tradesmen – ropers, gardener, laundress, woolcomber, painter and currier are among the occupations listed in 1854. By 1896 'white-collar' workers such as a public accountant, schoolmistresses and overseer of the poor had moved in while traders such as stonemason, rag merchant and cow keeper are still in evidence. South Street was so called because it was the only paved road leading south. It is one of only three of the ancient roads in Durham to be a street.

Durham, Old Elvet.

70. The name Elvet derives from 'Aelfet Ee' — swan island. Originally Old and New Elvet were areas, not streets. Old Elvet was the barony of Elvet around the Hallgarth (see 75) and New Elvet the borough developed about 1180 after the building of Elvet Bridge. Somewhat confusingly the areas 'exchanged' names in the 15th century which is why the main street of the 'newer' Elvet is designated Old Elvet. Unusually wide and spacious for Durham, Old Elvet is the finest street in the city. This part, near where the Elvets meet, was called Appii Forum and Three Taverns by Grammar School boys of the last century as it contained a trinity of taverns in which to sup beer. The fountain of 1863 in the foreground vanished before the Second World War and the Waterloo Hotel (extreme left) was demolished in the sixties.

OLD ELVET, DURHAM.

71. About 1925. A reverse view of no. 70, this photograph shows the prominent Royal County Hotel with the balcony from which on Miners' Day miners' leaders and politicians greet miners as they process to the University playing fields (2, 46). Beyond the County is the substantial front of the Waterloo Hotel, another victim of clearance prior to the road development of the sixties and seventies. Pattison's Temperance Hotel and café seen on the near side of the County have been incorporated into the County and much altered. Chapel Passage arch on the extreme right once led to the Georgian Methodist Chapel of 1808, which by the 1920s was the bakehouse for Alderman Pattison's café. Both chapel and arch have gone.

SHIRE HALL. DURHAM.

72. Now named 'Old Shire Hall', the Shire Hall stands in Old Elvet as a monument to the municipal pride and power of the late 19th century. It was designed in 1895 by two young local architects, Harry Barnes and Frederick Coates. Coates was also a pioneer designer of early motor cycles. Barnes became an M.P. and an advocate of slum clearance and municipal housing. Peter Lee, the miners' leader after whom Peterlee was named, was elected a Labour councillor in 1909 and 'practically lived in the Shire Hall'. In 1919 he became Chairman of Durham's first Labour County Council and a leading figure in the reform of housing and public services. The new 'County Hall' at Aykley Heads made Shire Hall redundant in 1963, and it became the administrative centre of the University.

MASONIC HALL, OLD ELVET, DURHAM.

73. Like the Shire Hall (72), but on a miniaturised scale, the Masonic Hall is somewhat incongruously placed among the plainer buildings nearby. It was designed by Charles Ebdy, the Lodge's architect, who was better known for his skill as a fisherman and as a writer on angling matters than as an architect. The new hall was built of the finest materials including dressed ashlar from the local Brasside quarries and polished red granite. The elaborate façade incorporated the 'all-seeing eye' together with the arms of the Duke of Zetland and of the Provincial Grand Master, John Fawcett, borne by carved rampant lions. The Hall's official opening in 1869 was marked by a great procession and a local holiday.

OLD ELVET DURHAM.

74. About 1925. The trees at the head of Old Elvet stand on virtually all that remains of the 'village green'. Facing them are houses with 18th and 19th century façades. Until the mid-1950s a horse fair was held twice a year in this area, and the serenity of the street was much disturbed by the clatter of hooves as the horses were made to show their paces, and by the sounds of Irish and gypsy accents. Until after the First World War these houses were pleasant family homes of the comfortably affluent, but most are now University or administrative buildings. The balcony behind the nearest lamp-post was said to have been erected to give a grandstand view of the public hangings at the goal opposite.

75. This little barn is the outstanding part of a small group of mediaeval buildings which most unexpectedly survive tucked away behind Hallgarth Street. They once belonged to the Prior's manor of Elvet, but now they are Crown property and used by Durham Prison. This barn has a stone ground floor, while its upper storey is timber framed. It now houses the Prison Officers' Club, surely one of the most unusual uses ever found for a monastic tithe barn.

76. A tranquil scene such as this suggests an isolated rural retreat; but the Cathedral tower and that of St. Oswald's indicate that this is in the Elvet area of Durham City, behind Hallgarth Street. On the right, added to an earlier outbuilding, is a gin-gan or horse gin. During the 19th century many County Durham farmers threshed their corn with a rotary machine driven by horse power. The horses had to walk around in circles and hexagonal buildings like this one at Hallgarth were added to many farm outbuildings to house the horse and the gin (i.e. engine).

77. Brown's Three Tuns Hotel still survives in New Elvet, and has been an inn for at least 130 years. Brown was the name of the proprietors during the latter part of the last century. A tun was a cask holding four hogsheads or 252 wine-gallons. Beyond the Three Tuns is the Cock Inn (78) and a taller building which when demolished a few years ago revealed a good 17th century staircase. Facing us is the County Court building in Old Elvet. Built in 1871 to the design of T.C. Sorby, it was of such fine stone that it was still as good as new over ninety years later when, together with the Waterloo Hotel next door, it was demolished to make way for the approach road to the new bridge.

78. This pair of old houses in New Elvet were once typical of Durham buildings (35). This was the Cock Inn. The upper bay still had its 18th century sliding small-paned windows and the downstairs window their wooden shutters. The inn was replaced by a building itself later demolished; the site is now the entrance to the car park of the Three Tuns (77).

79. About 1930. The staff of Thompsons Red Stamp Stores pose proudly outside their shop in New Elvet next door to the Three Tuns Hotel. The young women have the 'bobbed' hairstyle made fashionable by film stars and the 'bright young things' of the late 1920s. Thompsons' customers were given stamps when they bought groceries here and these could be exchanged for more goods when the stamp book provided by the store was full. The prices displayed appear ridiculously low. Their deceptive cheapness falls into perspective when one remembers that a labourer earnt about £1.10s.0d a week, if he was lucky enough to work a full week. The ballroom and conference suite of the Three Tuns now stand on this site.

80. Before the days of affluence and the cheap car, cycling was the working man's passport to freedom. Cycling clubs were very popular and bicycles a familiar sight. George Forster's cycle depot at 16 New Elvet was a local bicycle emporium for enthusiasts in the 1920s (45). The building no longer survives. Its position was roughly in the area of the present loading bay alongside the Three Tuns Hotel.

81. Joseph Johnson, brewer and maltster, had his City Brewery at 74 New Elvet in the 1890s. The Brewery, evidently a house before its change of use, had been a brewery at least forty years earlier when it was Bentham and Fenwick's brewery. The exact site of the City Brewery is not clear. It no longer survives. It was on the west side of New Elvet, an area which (apart from a few buildings at the north end) was completely demolished to make way for new University buildings.

NEVILLES CROSS DURHAM

82. Before 1886. Neville's Cross, erected in 1346 to commemorate a nearby victory against the Scots, was vandalised in 1589. Mutilated, it survived, but by the late 19th century it had become this sad relic, with a broken milestone inserted in its empty socket. In 1886 it was threatened with total destruction because of the 'eruption of red brick houses in the fields around it'. Henry Dodd, agent to the Weardale and Shildon Water Company, who lived nearby, organised its preservation. Moved to safety and encircled by railings it still stands somewhat overwhelmed by its surroundings. No longer do children chant as they did in Dodd's day: 'Walk nine times around the cross, lay your head to the turf, and you will hear the clash of arms and the noise of battle.'

SHINCLIFFE, NEAR DURHAM. C.H. T/C. 4256.

83. Shincliffe, about two miles from the city centre, is a pretty village with its tree-lined main street and 18th and early 19th century cottages bordering green verges. It retained its 'old world charm' until about 1960; since then it has become something of a dormitory village. There has been much modern in-fill and most of the cottages, extended and modernised, have moved 'up-market'. Wesley preached in the village, once from the stairs in Old Manor House and once in the open air. In 1950 a local family still treasured the lantern held over Wesley's head as he preached until after dark in the street shown in this picture of 1902.

BRANCEPETH VILLAGE.

84. Originally built in the mid-19th century as estate workers' cottages, these attractive stone houses at Brancepeth are now much in demand as 'desirable residences'. At the end of the broad drive leading to the Castle grounds are the fine entrance gates and in the background a glimpse of the neo–Norman towers of the Castle. Mature trees enhance the view and the whole vista shows how cleverly architects such as John Paterson and Anthony Salvin created the romanticized 'baronial scene' desired by their wealthy employers from the partially ruined mediaeval castle of the Nevilles. The following three cards illustrate other examples of romantic stage setting at Brancepeth.

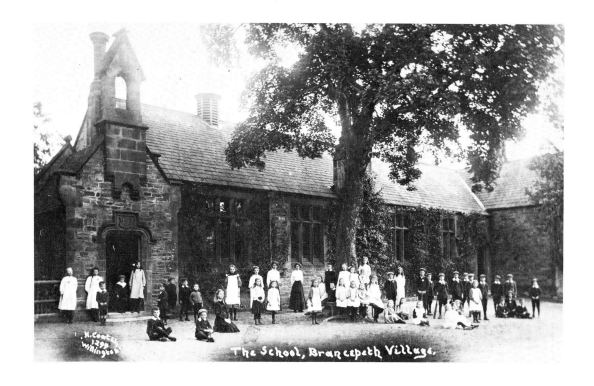

The School, Brancepeth Village.

85. This charming picture of the National School, Brancepeth, was taken about 1910. The school was one of the many mid-19th century improvements made to the estate by Emma Maria, the Russell heiress, and her husband, the 8th Viscount Boyne. Lord Boyne adopted the name of Russell and Brancepeth Castle was a major family residence until sold in 1922. The Boyne title was awarded to the 1st Viscount by William III for the prominent part he played in crushing Irish Roman Catholic support for James Stuart. The title 'Boyne' was chosen to commemorate the English victory at the Battle of the Boyne in 1690, the anniversary of which event is still the cause of unhappy sectarian rivalry in Ireland.

Barons Hall.

86. The Baron's Hall was created in the old Bulmer Tower largely by Charles Tennyson d'Eyncourt whose 'help' thoroughly exasperated Paterson, the official architect. Tennyson stage-managed William Russell's lying in state here in 1822. The Hall was draped in black, the only light allowed came from great candelabra which stood either side of the ornate coffin beneath a great black-plumed panoply; eight 'faithful retainers' kept watch day and night. A richly painted hatchment and other heraldic devices emphasized the 'feudal' character of the scene. It was all part of the romanticized mediaevalism which 'dissolved in the trenches of the First World War'. It is somewhat ironic therefore to see the Baron's Hall here equipped in 1917 as a ward for men wounded in those trenches.

87. No old English village was complete without a blacksmith and the 19th century 'improvers' of the Brancepeth estate built one with this fine horseshoe doorway in which the smith, Mr. R. Tindale, stands. There are still Tindales living in the village but the forge has not been worked for many years and was recently incorporated into a small 'executive' housing development. There are those who would argue that no old English village was complete without an inn. One will look in vain for this amenity in Brancepeth for the Russells did not allow one. However, beer for their own use was brewed, by the finest brewer in Durham!

The Smithy, Brancepeth.

88. Brancepeth Station once had a private waiting room for the Russells of Brancepeth Castle, who also had the privilege of halting trains on the line for unscheduled stops should members of the family or their guests wish to travel. The railway has long been closed and the track is now a public walk. The station buildings still survive; refurbished and extended, they are now part of a pleasant home.

89. This photograph is of St. Lawrence's Church, Pittington Hallgarth around 1880 when it was still lit by oil-lamps. The 'Pittingtons', four miles from the city centre, are a fascinating area well worth exploration. The first Pittington was Pittington Hallgarth, so called because of the Manor House or Hallgarth of the Priors of Durham established there around 1050. Of this early settlement only 'humps and bumps' north of the church (indicating traces of the manor) and St. Lawrence's itself remain. Skilful and sensitive enlargement in 1846/47 ensured that while much was new, much of the old remained, thus ensuring that the Hallgarth church retained its claim to be outstanding in a county of outstanding parish churches.

The Cartoons of the **Pittington Pictures.**

An Undergraduate of Durham University is seen here in 1888 copying the Mural Painting of St. Cuthbert. The artist eventually became a Bishop. Dr. Hamlyn (at one time Bishop of Accra) died suddenly January 20th, 1929. He had made this sketch in October, 1928, at my request (A.A.B.) See also Nos. 4 and 5.

No. 19.

90. The murals being copied depict two incidents from the life of St. Cuthbert: his consecration as Bishop, and the vision he had while dining at Whitby Abbey of a fellow monk's death. The paintings surround two deeply splayed windows set in the north wall of a church built just before the Norman Conquest. When the north aisle was built about 1190, this earlier wall was pierced to insert the exciting arcade of zig-zagged and chamfered arches supported by reeded and decorated piers. (Photo 1929.)

Photo by   Allan Burt.

Pittington's Historic Fonts.

1. Saxon Font restored to the Church after use as a Cattle Trough.
2. The Durham Cathedral Font (1663-1846). This White Marble Vase with carved Tudor cover was given to the Cathedral by Bishop Cosin. Eventually given by the Dean and Chapter to the " Mother Church of Durham," a larger font being placed in the Cathedral.

[Pittington Church No. 14.]

91. Although 'Pittington' has a Saxon derivation, earlier opinions that St. Lawrence's Church had a Saxon foundation are doubted by modern scholars, who suggest a date around 1033-1066, which would discount the claim of Pittington to be the 'Mother Church of Durham'. The description of the font cover as Tudor is also incorrect; it cost ten shillings in the late 17th century. This rare postcard shows not only the ancient font returned to the church eighty years after it had been sold to a local farmer for half-a-crown, but also the Cathedral font of 1663 given away in 1846 by Dean Waddington who thought it 'unsuitable' for the Cathedral. Dean Alington secured its return to the Cathedral in 1935.

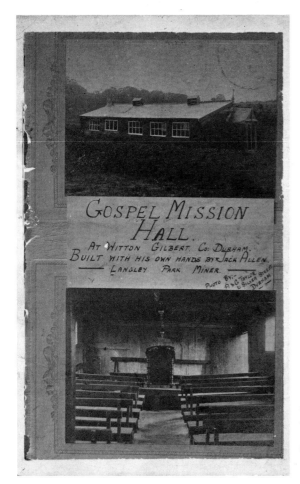

GOSPEL MISSION HALL.
AT WITTON GILBERT. CO. DURHAM.
BUILT WITH HIS OWN HANDS BY JACK ALLEN,
LANGLEY PARK. MINER.
PHOTO BY: A&G TAYLOR SILVER STREET DURHAM.

92. Witton Gilbert, 3½ miles west of Durham, became part of the city in 1974. Of Norman foundation, its lovely church still retains orginal features and a nearby farm has the remains of a leper hospital. In the 19th century, coal mining led to a rapid growth in the population of the village, from 417 in 1831 to 4,400 in 1891. This little Gospel Hall with its wooden benches was built in the village by a Langley Park miner, Jack Allen, shortly before the First World War. It is a humbling expression of a man's faith that, after working perhaps fifty hours a week in a dangerous job, he could face such a task. The Hall was pulled down in the early 1960s. (Photo 1914.)